24-Hour

Business Plan Template

24-Hour
Business Plan Template

How to Validate Your Startup Ideas and Plan Your Business Venture

STEVEN FIES

24-Hour Business Plan Template
How to Validate Your Startup Ideas and Plan Your Business Venture

Copyright © 2015 by Steven Fies

All rights reserved. With the exception of quotes used in reviews, this book may not be reproduced or used in whole or in part by any means existing without express written permission from Steven Fies.

Edited by Marian Kelly
Published by Steven Fies
United States of America

Electronic Edition: September 2015
Library of Congress Control No.: 2015914904
ISBN: 978-1517210991

"The Man in the Arena"

It is not the critic who counts; not the man who points out how the strong man stumbles, or where the doer of deeds could have done them better. The credit belongs to the man who is actually in the arena, whose face is marred by dust and sweat and blood; who strives valiantly; who errs, who comes short again and again, because there is no effort without error and shortcoming; but who does actually strive to do the deeds; who knows great enthusiasms, the great devotions; who spends himself in a worthy cause; who at the best knows in the end the triumph of high achievement, and who at the worst, if he fails, at least fails while daring greatly, so that his place shall never be with those cold and timid souls who neither know victory nor defeat.

-Theodore Roosevelt
From his famous speech, "Citizenship in a Republic"
April 23, 1910 in Paris, France

Table of Contents

I. ONLINE TOOLS	I
II. INTRODUCTION	3
III. HOW TO USE THIS BOOK	11
IV. THE IMPORTANCE OF VALIDATION	29
V. THE PLAN	33
1. COVER PAGE	35
2. EXECUTIVE SUMMARY	37
3. COMPANY OBJECTIVES	39
4. PRODUCTS & SERVICES	43
5. CUSTOMER ANALYSIS	45
6. COMPETITOR & INDUSTRY ANALYSIS	47
7. SALES & MARKETING STRATEGY	57
8. OPERATIONS & LOGISTICS	69
9. MANAGEMENT STRUCTURE	75
10. BUSINESS CAPITALIZATION	77
11. FINANCIAL PLAN	79
V. CONCLUSION	85

I. Online Tools

Welcome to the *24-Hour Business Plan Template: How to Validate Your Startup Ideas and Plan Your Business Venture*.

To accelerate the process for you, I've created a custom-built care package for you to download from my personal blog:

http://www.stevenfies.com/24-hour-business-plan-template

This free package was designed specifically to accompany this book. It includes a pre-formatted business plan template and cash-flow spreadsheet to get you started.

Before reading further, I'd recommend downloading this package and glancing quickly through the included resources.

Note that these files have been adapted from the ones I used myself when making the transition from full-time employment to full-time business ownership and entrepreneurship.

II. Introduction

Welcome to the 24-Hour Business Plan Template.

Let me explain exactly what I mean by "24-hour."

It may take you more or less than twenty-four hours to create your business plan, but I've chosen this amount of time (twenty-four hours) as your *baseline target* for a reason.

I want to cement the idea that you should keep a relatively fast pace at this stage.

The initial planning process cannot and should not take forever.

While it's true that businesses must be carefully engineered, please realize it may take you a few tries to "get it right" with your business plan - and you want to get through that trial and error phase as quickly as possible.

After all, you could all too easily spend six to twelve months crafting one "perfect plan," only to realize deep into the process that it's not as perfect as you once thought. It'd be a real shame to spend so much time only to realize you're back at square one.

By moving at a quicker pace, you can speed up the strategic process and reach the critical point of action sooner. Failures, oversights, and imperfections will all matter far less because the investment will be less, and no matter what happens, you accelerate your learning curve.

Author Eric Ries discusses this in his popular book *The Lean Startup*, a favorite of entrepreneurs and startup junkies everywhere.

He calls it "failing forward fast."

In short, this principle states that you should test core product concepts as quickly as possible because the quicker you can get through an "iteration" - test a certain idea, method, or strategy - the faster you can find out if it's viable or not.

He discusses this in the context of product development, but the underlying principle applies to any scenario where you're operating under uncertainty.

Let's put this into context: you might need to create seven business plans before finally arriving at *one* that's viable and executable.

This is true whether you're fiddling with the same core business idea in seven different ways or playing with seven completely different ideas altogether.

No matter the case, if each iteration takes you several months, then it will be many years before you ever get off the ground. This would be impractical and result in significant time lost without any real headway.

By contrast, if each iteration only takes you twenty-four hours (or even a few days or weeks), you'll be up and running in a matter of weeks or months, which is more reasonable.

There are some of you who will internalize this more easily than others.

So-called "perfectionists" (not unlike myself!) are the ones who need to be careful. If this describes you, beware of your tendency to delay things until they're "perfect."

Here's why:

Deep down, you may want to hold off on taking action on your business plan until you have more information, more analysis, etc.

The danger of such a mindset is twofold:

1. You'll never get anywhere if you always delay because you're afraid things aren't perfect.

2. Taking action on your plan (going "into the arena") is truly the *only* source of objective information and analysis. For better or worse, you can't argue with real-world results.

With regard to the latter point, think on it long and hard. To get the information and analysis you seek, you need to escape the theoretical confines of your mind and **get out into the real world**.

No matter how brilliant you may be, there is no substitute for practical and meaningful real-life data.

Real-life data allows you to observe and measure what's actually happening and make sense of it.

Whether you succeed or fail in a given trial run or "iteration," you're guaranteed to *learn* and *progress* from the experience - and over time, consistent progress increases your ability to succeed.

To not use real-life data is to guess, hypothesize, and (perhaps) succumb to information paralysis - due to too much or too little information - and get nowhere.

If you've ever dwelled on what "might" or "could" happen "if" action was taken, then you know what I'm talking about. This type of thinking tends to promote anxiety and basically accomplishes nothing.

Here's a quick test to see if this is you:

How many times in your life have you dismissed an idea purely on a theoretical basis (maybe it doesn't "seem" likely, or something doesn't feel like it equates) without having actually tested it?

"That diet wouldn't work for me."

"Why would I go say hi? That girl/guy is out of my league; she/he wouldn't be into me..."

"That's impossible."

But how do you *really* know if these things are true without testing them?

To illustrate how ridiculous this type of thinking is, consider a few examples from the past:

- In 1876, Alexander Graham Bell (inventor of the first successful telephone) attempted to sell his patent for the device to Western Union for $100,000. They rejected the offer, claiming the telephone simply *"wasn't capable of transmitting recognizable speech over several miles."*
- In 1880, the Stevens Institute of Technology publically proclaimed that Thomas Edison's light bulb would never work.
- In 1901, Wilbur Wright thought it would be fifty years before we could make airplanes that would fly. It was only two years later in 1903 that he and his brother, Orville, had their first successful flight.
- In 1913, a U.S. District Attorney actually prosecuted Lee De Forest (an inventor involved in the development of AM radio) for selling stock in his radio company, saying he was a fraud for indicating we were on the verge of transmitting the human voice across the ocean.
- In 1926, Lee De Forest himself shot down the idea that television would ever exist, saying, *"while theoretically and technically television may be feasible, commercially and financially it is an impossibility, a*

development of which we need waste little time dreaming."

These are just a few examples, and the last is particularly thought provoking. Here's an inventor who was sued on the basis that he was a fraud for claiming radios could work, and now *he's* the one saying we'll never have television!

Realize: most or all of these things seemed improbable during their time of conception – but they *were* possible and *did* come to pass.

Many times, we simply don't know the truth of something until we have developed and tested it thoroughly.

Plus, this goes to show you that *all* of us (even the innovators!) are prone to making errors in judgment or falling victim to that which we call "assumption."

People used to think the world was flat, after all.

The lesson here is simple.

While you need to put deep thought into any business endeavor, you must also balance it with appropriate *action and advancement* - these will be the real, objective tests of viability.

You will likely encounter some failures along the way, because that's the nature of refining an idea and getting to the bottom of things, but these are to be embraced for the learning and advancement they provide.

Remember to stay optimistic, even while you manage and maintain realistic expectations.

Great things often start with a strong and powerful vision, and you'll need some faith and belief to pursue your dream with the vigor required to succeed.

This starts with your business plan and continues into the operating and growth stages of your business. It is a continual journey.

Please keep all of this in mind as you read this book.

What I've provided for you in the chapters that follow (as well as on my website, in the form of supplementary materials) is a relatively simple and traditional business plan - simple enough, hopefully, that you can get through it at the fast pace I recommend.

What makes the information in this book powerful, though, isn't the relative level of simplicity or the efficiency of the content. Rather, it's *what you do with it*.

You can use this information as a source of inspiration and take prompt, methodical action towards your goals, or you can sit back and do nothing.

The choice is yours.

At the very least, I'd recommend you do *something*, even if it isn't perfect or up to your ideal standards.

This is why I've started this book with a disclaimer that you should keep a brisk pace and a brief look into the psychology of perfectionism and assumptive thinking (so you can stay objective and avoid getting caught up in your head and failing to take action).

At the end of the day, these are needle-moving factors that will make a difference for you when you start your business - and presumably that's what you're planning to do if you're reading this book.

Now - hopefully I've nudged you into the right frame of mind to move forward and succeed with this.

For additional information, please find me on my blog at www.stevenfies.com. Best of luck to you!

III. How to Use This Book

I designed this book to give you a simple, no-nonsense way to create a viable business plan in a short amount of time – approximately twenty-four hours.

You might be wondering, "Can this really be done?"

Absolutely.

In fact, you can pump out a solid business plan in even less time. We've all heard stories of someone making a few scribbles on the back of a napkin at a restaurant and then going on to create a multi-million dollar enterprise.

Things may not work out that way for everybody, but the napkin business plan illustrates a key point – as significant as your written business plan is, your *vision* and *follow-through* are twenty times more important.

Realize: you don't need to plan *every* little detail before getting started. In reality, most new businesses undergo so much change in the first several months (or even years) of operation that the plan itself must adapt and change throughout that time anyway.

It would be far too easy to spend months planning, perfecting, and polishing a plan that never sees the light of day because you fail to execute it (please don't fall victim to this mistake) or because you still haven't taken the time to *validate* the core concept.

Validation

The faster you can validate your core business concept (or *invalidate* it and move on), the better. You really can't afford to spend months on a plan, only to find out that there's no market for your product or service, so be sure to figure this out up front.

How do you go about validating your core business concept quickly and effectively?

Many business school professors will tell you to run *surveys* – i.e., get out there and ask *real* people if they would buy your product.

One way to do this involves hiring a professional market research company to administer surveys to your target market in order to find out the likelihood that they will buy your product and at what price.

There's also no shame in standing on a busy street corner or visiting a street fair and asking strangers as they pass by – plus, this method has the advantage of being free (except for your time, of course).

Likewise, you can stand on a "virtual" street corner by asking members of online forums what they think of your idea. Reddit.com is a good starting point, as are niche-specific forums related to your business.

Friends, family, mentors, colleagues, and peers also make for great sounding boards. You can even take to social media, such as Facebook, to ask your network what they think of a particular idea; you'll likely get a number of responses and comments in a short order.

As outsiders looking in, these people can see the things you've overlooked better than you can, and they'll give you a valuable perspective on your business prospects.

By the way, some new entrepreneurs are afraid to conduct market research and share their ideas for fear they will be stolen. Don't be – aside from the fact it's unlikely someone will suddenly drop everything in their life to pursue your idea, you should be more afraid of what will happen if you invest substantial time and money into an idea that's untested and unproven.

Now, I'll give you one final method to consider when validating your business idea. This won't apply to every business model, but it can be effective in situations where it does apply.

The Fake Sales Page

If you have the money, this method involves "selling" the product before it's ever made.

This particular strategy works best for online products or businesses, and was originally introduced to me by Richard of realpassiveincome.com. There are some other versions of this method floating around the internet, too, and you can find them easily enough if you do a few searches. A version of this method is also referenced in the book *Traction* by Gabriel Weinberg and Justin Mares, which we will discuss again in Chapter 7.

Here's how it works:

In this scenario, you create a fake sales page online with your to-be product listed, and then send traffic to it using PPC (pay-per-click) ads, social media ads, or another chosen traffic channel, making sure to aim the ads at your target market.

Your sales page will have a "buy now" button, and you will measure what percentage of people click on this button after landing on your page from the ads. Conversion rates of 5-10% or more (meaning 5-10% of the people who came to your page clicked the "buy now" button) are promising. Anything less than this and you're probably barking up the wrong tree.

At this point you can probably already see the value in doing this. With minimal effort, you can see if people will buy your product or service *before* you go to all the trouble of actually creating it – saving you lots of time and money in the long run.

Now, you might be wondering what happens after someone clicks the "buy now" button. One strategy involves passing them through to a second page that explains the product is coming soon (or is in development), and inviting them to join your email list for updates.

Note: this doubles as a great way to get in touch with your customer base and ask them questions about what would make your product, service, or business more valuable.

You might also be wondering exactly how much web traffic you need in order to validate your conversion rate information (verify that it's statistically significant). Many of my peers will tell you an ad budget of $250-500 is more than enough, and they're probably right. If you don't see any signs of traction after investing this amount of money, it's likely not worth investing more.

Consider also that, depending on your niche market, the number of eyes you can drive to your page for $250-500 will differ. At a cost to you of $0.50 per click, you might get 500-1,000 people to your page, whereas at $3.70 per click, you might find that you can barely scrape up 100 test subjects.

Because of this, I would normally recommend avoiding creating products or services (or businesses for that matter) in a niche where the cost-per-click is already high, because it signifies that a lot of competition already exists.

It will naturally be easier to choose a niche where competition is lower, as is your cost per click for testing purposes. Plus, choosing a niche with a lower cost per click for ads has the advantage of giving you a greater sample size due to sheer mathematics, as discussed above.

In layman's terms, this means your ad experiment results will be more meaningful and trustworthy. When the conversion rate from a group of 500-1,000 people is measured, you can have greater confidence in your findings than you can in the results from a smaller group of just 100 people.

That being said, there is nothing wrong with choosing a more competitive niche. You just need to be prepared for what that means in terms of both testing and your potential business opportunities in the long run – you'll have a steeper mountain to climb.

Also, keep in mind that you may need to run several of these tests before you find a particular idea that "works."

Whether you test a bunch of different ideas or the same basic idea packaged up and sold a bunch of different ways, it pays to do the testing up front. Otherwise, you could spend a ton of time and money developing a product that will never sell.

Many entrepreneurs, authors, musicians, bloggers, and other creative people fall victim to this every day. I myself have fallen victim to it multiple times in my life, and I might even fall victim to it again in the future if I'm not careful.

Why?

It's easy to get caught up in the passion and excitement of an idea and want to create it and bring it to life. But speaking from experience, it's never fun to launch your creations into the world to the sound of crickets.

Thus, even if it seems like a hassle to invest a few hundred bucks in the beginning to do some market research, you should do it. It pays dividends in the long run and keeps you from investing massive quantities of blood, sweat, and tears (and money!) into ideas that have a low probability of success.

Now let's assume that you've arrived at a point where you have done a few ad experiments and you've stumbled across an idea that appears to be working: your conversion rate is a whopping 11.3% and you're feeling great! What happens next?

You could stop here, but you might be better off going one step further, using A/B split testing to drill deeper into your market research. In the case of a book, this might involve testing different titles; in the case of a product, perhaps you could try offering it in two different colors to see which is more popular. The possibilities are endless.

No matter what you're selling, you might also consider A/B testing the price point to see where you will be most profitable. Maybe on your original sales page, you listed a price of $99; now you can try A/B testing a second price of $198 for the exact same product or service.

Now let's say when you try this higher price, you notice that your conversion rate drops from 11.3% to 6.4%. This drop might seem like a detriment at first, but when you do the math, you're actually coming out ahead.

How?

Simple: even though you are driving fewer sales, your price has doubled. Hence, as long as your conversion rate hasn't dropped by more than half, you will still make more money. 6.4% is exactly 56.63% of 11.3% in this example, so you are better off at the higher price.

You may have other reasons for keeping your price at a certain point (high *or* low), even if a different price appears to be more profitable – and that's okay.

Perhaps you want to use a lower price because having a greater volume of customers is important for strategic purposes. Or maybe you want to maintain a higher price so as not to decrease the perceived value of your advertised product or service. Individual circumstances may vary.

Regardless of the case, know that you can empower yourself by accumulating this type of information in advance.

By the way, I realize we all have a different level of expertise when it comes to web development and running online ads. For some of you, this will all be very easy – you'll be able to setup a sales page, send traffic to it, and track conversions without much effort. If that's the case – great!

On the other hand, you may not have the first clue where to start. The technical elements of building a website, tracking real-time events via analytics tools, and creating ad campaigns are beyond the scope of this book, but feel free to contact me at www.stevenfies.com if you need help.

Keep in mind, too, that you can still use traditional surveys to obtain much of the same information you'd get from running online ads and measuring the results. This web-based method is just one way to slice the pie; the underlying principles can be extrapolated and applied in a number of different ways and through other channels.

The important thing is that you do *something* to obtain *measurable feedback* from real people (to make sure you're on the right track) before getting deep into product development.

More on validation in the next section.

What This Book Isn't

Let's be clear on what this book is not. This book is not a promise that you will be successful, nor is it a promise that you'll be able to *launch* your business in twenty-four hours.

In regards to the first statement, your success is entirely in your hands. The market always has a need (read: economic demand) for some product or service, and you're more likely to succeed if you form your business around something that's actually in demand. Again, the importance of validation cannot be overstated.

In regards to the second statement, implementation (launching your business, then continuing to manage it on an ongoing basis) simply takes time.

When I decided to go into business for myself full-time in early 2015, my business plan was completed during one particularly focused weekend, but it took several months to *implement* it – and then walk away from my full-time job and open shop.

There were three reasons for this.

First, I wanted to remain with my employer for a period of time to save additional money before making the transition. Specifically, my goal was to save enough to have a full 1-2 year "ramp" to get my business off the ground.

Second, my business partner and I shared the desire to pick up a few clients prior to moving forward – both for purposes of validation and to obtain some positive references.

Third, there were professional certifications to obtain, bank accounts to open, documents to file with the Secretary of State, partnership agreements to execute, and a minimum viable website to be built for the grand opening.

Some might argue these last "official" steps weren't necessary at this early stage, but they made sense in the context of the arrangement with my business partner. We also happen to be in B2B software and consulting, so having a basic website for clients to view was important (speaking of which, feel free to find us online at www.thinkplanlaunch.com).

In summary, each of these steps took time despite the fact that my plan was clear from the beginning.

Your idea may take more or less time to implement than mine did, and that's perfectly okay – just remember to spend the appropriate time validating your idea in the beginning. Otherwise, you might proceed forward with an idea that won't work!

As you move forward with this book, continue to remind yourself that it's better to cycle through several business ideas in a short span of time – and in doing so, determine their viability – than to spend all your time perfecting one plan that you never take action on, or to invest in an idea that wasn't objectively researched in the beginning.

Here is a specific planning process you can use to stay on track:

The 7-Step Guide to Planning Your Business in Twenty-four Hours

1. First, spend some time brainstorming potential business ideas. You may already be decided on a particular idea, in which case you can move on to the next step. Otherwise, write down anything that comes to mind and make note of the ideas that seem most promising. Try to complete this step in no more than two hours.

2. Now, take the most promising idea from Step 1 and complete the following tasks:
    a. Identify your product(s) and/or service(s). (Ch. 4)
    b. Identify your target market/customer. (Ch. 5)
    c. Evaluate the industry and competitors. (Ch. 6)
    d. Identify your sales and marketing strategy. (Ch. 7)

    Try to complete this step in no more than two hours.

    It is particularly indicative of a solid plan when the answers to these questions are very clear and easy to come up with. For example:

    "My product is an app that coordinates pizza deliveries. My target market is 18-to-36-year-olds who live in densely populated cities – and I know this because research shows they order pizza more often than most people. My competitors include similar app companies, like Favor, that offer on-demand

delivery services, but despite the competition, there is room for more such businesses because the market is growing. We plan to find our first customers through non-scalable, local grass-roots marketing and will expand to other traction channels, such as Public Relations, SEM (Search Engine Marketing), and Trade Shows, as soon as we obtain VC funding."

As you can see, this is quite clear and shows that you have a solid understanding of the core business.

When your answers aren't quite so clear, it often spells trouble and means you don't yet have an actionable plan.

After all, it's hard to bring a product or service to market if you don't know what it is, who it's for, where your competition is, or how it will be sold and marketed. For example:

"I want to make software apps. My target market is everybody, because everybody will love them. I'm not really sure who my competitors are, but everyone likes apps, right? I'll hire someone to handle sales and marketing."

This is a bit of an extreme example, but you get the idea – and you can see the stark contrast between this example and the prior one. The prior one is very clear, specific, and to the point, which is required for your plan to be actionable.

Note: should you find at any point during your research that your plan does not seem viable or cannot be clarified to an actionable level, scrap it and start over.

3. Next, you will:
    a. Determine your basic logistical and operational plan. (Ch. 8)
    b. Decide your management structure. (Ch. 9)
    c. Identify how the business will be funded (called "capitalization"). (Ch. 10)
    d. Identify how the business will manage its finances in the early stages and through its initial growth, and how you will survive while running the business (will you draw a salary, live off your savings, work a second job during the startup stage, or keep your job and start your business in your spare time?). (Ch. 11) Try to complete this step in no more than <u>four hours</u>.

4. Now, **create a life plan** for yourself, one that specifies *exactly what will happen next*, every day and every week, all the way up to the point of launching your business.
    If you're not used to using a calendar, schedule, or some other method for organizing your life, this may

take you some time. The important thing is to work *backwards* from the projected launch date of your business, asking yourself at each step *what needs to happen just prior to this step* and *how much time it will realistically take*.

With these questions answered, you can construct a simple and effective action timeline.

Once your timeline is complete, digest it for a few minutes and think about what this will mean for your life.

Will you be leaving your job? Borrowing money? Moving across the country or world?

How many weeks, months, or years before your estimated launch date?

Try to complete Step 4 in no more than <u>four hours</u>.

Be sure you're prepared to commit to the required steps of your life plan before moving forward. If you aren't, it's time to scrap this plan and start over.

5. Now that you've brainstormed the basic framework for your business and are prepared to move forward, it's time to **validate your idea**, as discussed previously in this section (and in the next section – IV. The Importance of Validation).
This is the part where you'll research and survey your market, ask friends and family for their

opinions, and potentially even set up a fake sales page to test conversion rates on incoming traffic.

Note: some might argue that validation should be Step 1 instead of Step 5. However, I would argue that in order to pursue validation, you first need to have a basic grip on your product, target market, industry, and business strategy (as discussed in the steps above). Otherwise, you might not know how to position your product, who to survey, or what questions to ask when seeking validation.

That being said, feel free to start validation sooner than Step 5 if you feel sufficiently prepared. Generally speaking, the faster you can prove or disprove a given business idea, the better.

Try to take no more than <u>eight hours</u> for this step.

6. Once you've validated your business idea, you should finish your business plan. In addition to drafting and formatting the information you've already researched (Chapters 4-11), you will draft your cover page, type your executive summary, and summarize your company objectives (Chapters 1-3). Try to complete this step in no more than <u>four hours</u>.

7. Finally, **execute and follow through** – and feel free to modify your plan as needed along the way. Flexibility is important, after all.

In Summary

Let me remind you that it's perfectly okay if this process takes you longer (or shorter!) than twenty-four hours.

Please just realize that the longer the planning process drags out, the longer it will be before you take action, and the longer before you reach your goal.

In summary:

1. **Brainstorm your big idea(s).** (2 hrs)
2. **Identify your product, customer, competition, and sales/marketing strategy.** (2 hrs)
3. **Identify your plan for operations, management, capitalization, and finances.** (4 hrs)
4. **Create a life plan.** (4 hrs)
5. ***Validate* your business idea.** (8 hrs)
6. **Type up your finished business plan.** (4 hrs)
7. **Execute and follow through on your plan.**

IV. The Importance of Validation

Starting a new business venture is exciting, and the process of doing the paperwork is rather simple when the time comes.

What is not quite as simple for most new entrepreneurs is *validating* their business idea before diving into the startup phase.

We discussed this in the previous section, and now we'll take a look at key questions to ask yourself and your peer/survey group(s) when performing validation research on your idea.

Key validation questions to ask:

- **Who is my target customer?** What age, what gender, what sorts of things do they do in their free time, etc.? Why would they buy your product? Get granular with this – you need to know who you're going to sell to in order to be successful.

- **Is there sufficient demand for my product or service in the open market?** (Will people actually buy this from my business?) Start by exploring whether or not the market is already buying similar products or services – if so, at least you know there is some validated demand already. If not, you will likely need to survey a large number of people in your established target market to find out if they will buy your innovative new product or not.

Friends, family, colleagues, and peers can often help with this – but you'll also want to get out into the "real world" and ask your true target audience. Remember, one tactical method for doing this involves by "selling" the product before it's ever made (as discussed last chapter). This costs money but provides you with valuable, objective data that you can use to evaluate your business concept.

Note: gauging the level of customer demand is possibly the most important part of the validation process. You may think you've struck gold with a brilliant business idea, but will quickly be humbled if you determine nobody is prepared to pay for it. Be sure you find out *how much* your customers are willing to pay, too, lest your costs of production and delivery exceed what you'll earn in revenue.

- **Do I have a sales channel that can be accessed and leveraged without high barriers to entry (or if there *are* barriers, do I have a plan to address them)?** This will be specific to each industry, so it's hard for me to point you to a specific website or resource to research this, but you can start with a quick google search and end by contacting an entrepreneur or business person who is in your field and can testify to how easy or difficult it was to get started.

Common barriers to entry include insufficient access to capital, high marketing costs, exclusive distribution agreements, resource monopolization, customer loyalty/brand recognition, predatory pricing, inelastic demand, legal issues, government regulations, and network effects.

- **Are there a significant number of competitors pursuing market share, and if so, what competitive advantages will allow me to meet this challenge?** The U.S. Census publishes a plethora of information that can aid you in answering this question (start here: http://www.census.gov/econ/isp/). You can also google your keywords and see what businesses are showing up near the top of the search results (i.e., "San Diego Plumber" or "New York Management Consultant"). Here again, speaking with an entrepreneur who is in the field can be extremely beneficial, and you may even get a mentor out of it if you're nice to them.

With these questions and the others that will arise during the course of planning your business, the key is to *take the time to think these through* and be sure you can answer them with enough confidence to bet your money on those answers.

It's too easy to skip over these seemingly simple questions. But therein lays the value of validating a business idea in the first place. *Taking the time to critically evaluate* your product or service, customers, competitors, pricing, barriers to entry, financial plan, and related factors will help ensure you're moving in the right direction.

V. The Plan

In the chapters that follow, I have created one chapter for each "section" of the business plan.

For example, Chapter 1 is the Cover Page, Chapter 2 is the Executive Summary, Chapter 3 is Company Objectives, and so on.

Each chapter serves as a *template* for the corresponding section of your business plan and also includes a brief *explanation* of how to research and write each section.

Remember that you can access a blank business plan template that corresponds to the layout of this book on my website at:

http://www.stevenfies.com/24-hour-business-plan-template

Now let's dive in and move forward together!

1. Cover Page

The cover page can be done first or last, since it's basically a "gimme." It comes first in this book simply because I've chosen to lay out the book in the same order as an actual business plan.

This page should feature your company logo and/or name centered in the middle of the page. Keep it simple, professional, and designed to grab attention right off the bat.

Steven Fies

2015 Business Plan

2. Executive Summary

The executive summary should be written last, and it is perhaps the most important part of your business plan if you are pitching it to investors or bankers.

It should cover your business idea, products and services, target market, and goals – touching on the key points from the other sections of your plan.

The reason it needs to be written last is because you will likely make adjustments to everything else along the way.

There is no sense crafting the perfect executive summary in the beginning, only to change it later because other elements of your plan need adjusting.

The key to this is being efficient, after all.

Your executive summary is a bit like a job resume and should be:

- **Clear, to the point, and easy to understand.** No technical jargon here – save anything ultra-complex for the detailed sections later.

- **Positive, upbeat, and lively!** It should convey your enthusiasm for the promise of your business.

- **Honest.** There is no need to inflate, overstate, or dress things up here, and frankly, if you find yourself needing to do so – whether to convince investors *or* yourself of a doubtful plan – you would be far better served by simply re-working the elements of your plan to make it truly strong.

- **Brief.** This is a "summary," after all. There are still plenty of pages that follow in which you can cover detail. Ideally, the executive summary will be in the one- to two-page range, certainly no more than three pages.

Remember to include:

- The **names of the owners** of the business.
- The **location**(s) of the business.
- **Startup capital required** to launch and a brief description of how it will be used.
- A **rough timeline** for the business, including estimated launch date, growth milestones, and a brief description of what things will look like five to ten years down the road.

3. Company Objectives

To put the purpose of this section into context, imagine something with me for a second:

When you shop for something online, the first thing you usually see on a product page (next to or below the picture) is the product description. This is a lot like the Executive Summary we discussed in Chapter 2.

There will also normally be a "specs" or technical detail section that you can click on for quick facts about the product. That's what this section, *Company Objectives*, is all about. It provides quick, important facts related to your business in an easily digestible format.

You are free to add to this list, but at a minimum, you will need to include the following:

- **Mission Statement**
    - This is a one- to three-sentence statement that describes the company's main focus. It should answer the question, "What is the purpose of this business, and why is it being formed?"

- **Guiding Principles**
    - What values, causes, and principles does your business stand behind?

- **Owners & Legal Structure**
    - Who will own this business and in what percentage(s)? What type of legal form will the business entity take: C-Corporation, S-Corporation, LLC, Sole Proprietorship, Benefit Corporation, Non-Profit Corporation, General Partnership...?

- **Industry**
    - List your NAICS code here, along with your primary industry. You can list a secondary industry if it makes sense (for example: Manufacturing → Plastics). [More info on NAICS codes and small business information can be found here: http://www.sba.gov/content/north-american-industry-classification-system-codes-and-small-business-size-standards]

- **Brief Review of Products, Services, & Customer Profile**
    - Since these will all be covered in more detail later in your business plan, do your best to keep this summary concise. For instance, *"XYZ Corp. will sell warehoused musical instruments at wholesale prices to universities and schools."*

- **Primary Business Objectives**
    - These are the top-level goals and accompanying milestones that the business will work towards over the next several years. If there are several, choose only the Top 3 for this section. I.e.,
        - *Establish ten new customer accounts by end of Year One, with $50,000.00 in monthly revenue.*
        - *Open second brick-and-mortar location and launch online operations by the end of Year Three, or sooner if monthly revenue exceeds $100,000.00 for at least six months.*
        - *Pay off business loan in full by end of Year Five; hire an executive manager and administrative assistant.*

- **Consolidated Financial Forecast**
    - Includes the total amount of capital required to start the business, expected monthly operating expenses and revenues, the amount of the monthly payment in the event of a bank loan, and estimated time to repay the bank and/or investors. Just the quick bullet points, no need for a lot of information here.

4. Products & Services

This is where you get to dive in and spend some real time describing *what* it is your business is selling, whether a product, service, or both.

Photos, drawings, and blueprints may be included here to help facilitate understanding of your products and services.

Be sure to include information regarding how your product or service creates value for your target customer. Include price detail and list any competitive advantages or disadvantages of your products and services compared to market alternatives.

To be sure you cover all the key points for each product and/or service, answer the following elementary questions in detail:

- **WHAT** is it?
- **WHO** will buy it?
- **WHY** will they buy it?
- **WHEN** will they use it?
- **WHERE** will they use it?
- **HOW** does it stack up against market substitutes (competing products)?

This section may be as long or short as it needs to be, depending on how many products or services you have.

If your business is something like an eCommerce store, with hundreds or thousands of products, it will suffice to provide a summary of the *types* of products you sell, along with some information regarding the features of your sales portal (the "service" part of your sales model). In this instance, the website itself would be considered the "service" that connects your customers with your products.

Similarly, if your small business will be centered around something informational, like a blog, your articles and any premium giveaways or extras could be listed here as "free products/services" alongside your paid products and services.

5. Customer Analysis

Keep this simple but be sure to spend adequate time answering the following questions.

Part 1:

- In one sentence, who is your customer?
- What is their demographic profile (age, location, interests, etc.)?
- Where do your customers get information about products and services like yours?
- Where is your average customer employed? Be specific – include the type of industry they work in, if applicable, along with their job title and function.
- What does your customer do in their free time?
- What guiding principles, beliefs, and values does your customer hold?
- Describe the average day in the life of your customer.

Part 2:

- List six reasons your customer *will* buy your products and services.
- List twelve reasons your customer *will not* buy your products and services. (That's right – come up with at least twelve objections your customer might have when considering a purchase!)

- What is the strongest single reason a customer will make a purchase?
- What is the most common objection you expect to face?
- Will the *will-buy* factors be able to overcome the *won't-buy* factors? Why or why not? If not, it's time to either A) target a different customer, or B) adjust the product, service, or business model to arrive at an affirmative response.

6. Competitor & Industry Analysis

Two extremely critical matters to consider when embarking on a new business venture are *Competitor* and *Industry* factors. Let's break these down individually.

Competitor factors are self-explanatory – someone else has already opened shop doing what you plan to do, and you need to figure out how big of a threat their existing activity poses to your business.

Industry factors include the big, over-arching movements in your market. These are make-or-break factors that you *and* your competitors have little to no control over, but which will affect all of your businesses.

To understand the difference between industry and competitor factors, I'll use the sport of surfing as a metaphor here.

Surfing as a Metaphor for Industry and Competitor Factors

When I lived in San Diego, I used to surf often. If surfing were a "business," the waves would have been my *customers*. My *competitors* were the other surfers out in the water, fighting for the same waves (customers) as me.

The more surfers there were in the water at any given time, the fewer waves there were to go around – and we would say the competition was *fierce*.

Notably, some surfers were more aggressive than others about pursuing waves; many would go so far as to "drop in" on a wave another surfer was already surfing, much like stealing someone's existing customer.

(Fortunately, most surfers in San Diego were kind enough to respect the "lineup" or branch off into temporary "territories" to establish a sense of order and sharing. This is more unlikely to occur in the business world.)

Now, regardless of how aggressive my competitors were in the water, *we all lost the game when the ocean itself failed to produce waves*.

Notice here how the ocean represents the *industry*, carrying the ability to make or break the market.

Some days, the ocean produces plenty of great waves for everyone; on other days, the ocean is dead and flat – and it's hard to do much if the ocean is flat (no market = no demand = no customers).

Therefore, regardless of the number of surfers in the water, the very first thing most surfers do before paddling out is look at the surf report. This helps us determine if it's even worth our time to drive to the beach (enter the market).

Assuming the surf report looks good enough to make the drive down to the beach, the second step is to evaluate our competition.

If the shoreline is heavily crowded with competing surfers, we know our prospects for catching waves might be bleak. We may reason that we should move on to another, less-crowded area, or drive to a different beach altogether.

However, sometimes it's still worth paddling out into a crowd if we feel our individual *competitive advantages* are strong enough to catch waves despite the competition – namely, superior physical fitness and the ability to read, catch, and ride waves.

It is much the same in business – a little observation and evaluation up front can provide the information needed to make better decisions.

***

You can see why I picked this analogy, and the key takeaways are simple.

First and foremost, you need to *ensure your customer base exists* within your industry; then, you must *evaluate your competition* to come up with a realistic assessment of your sales prospects.

This includes not only the *quantity* of competitors in your market, but also the *quality* of your competitors – what are their competitive advantages and disadvantages?

Do the other businesses "in the water" have advantages that make it more likely for them to "catch waves" (customers), making your success more difficult?

If so, is there another area (a different market segment or even another industry altogether) where you stand a better chance?

You get the idea.

As simple as this idea is, many new entrepreneurs fail to look at the surf report before driving down to the beach. Then, when they finally "get to the beach" to evaluate their prospects, they underestimate their competition and get frustrated when they don't catch any waves.

To avoid this common pitfall, take the following steps:

Industry Analysis

1. Before diving into any detailed statistics or data, *define* the specific metrics you will review and compare so you don't wind up in "analysis paralysis" (endlessly paging through data without ever reaching a stopping point). Some key metrics to dig into:

    a. **Market Size** ($)

    b. **Market Growth** – Past one year, past five years, past ten years (%)

c. **Market Demand** – What factors might increase or decrease demand over the next several years and why? If the economy as a whole changes, how might your business be affected?

d. **Market Trends** – What's happening with technological advancement, consumer preferences, new products, etc.?

e. **Barriers to Entry** – What barriers will you face and how will you overcome them? Common barriers to entry include insufficient access to capital, high marketing costs, exclusive distribution agreements, resource monopolization, customer loyalty/brand recognition, predatory pricing, inelastic demand, legal issues, government regulations, and network effects.

2. Then get the information you need to analyze these metrics through **secondary research** (data, statistics, and studies from sources like the Census Bureau and Small Business Administration.) Take advantage of the many statistical and data-reporting sources available via USA.gov. Additionally:

    a. Consider visiting the library and reviewing the *Statistical Abstract of the United States* and the

Encyclopedia of Associations. (Plus, tell the librarian what you're doing and see what their recommendations are as to additional resources).

b. Access information from industry trade associations if available, including trade journals and compiled market data. Even if basic statistics are not available for free to the general public, many associations are willing to release them to a potential new trade member.

c. It goes without saying you should use Google as a resource and spend several hours reading up about market research – including the identification of specific sources of market information for *your* industry or niche.

3. Finally, move on to **primary research** (the gathering of market information from your target customers). This type of information is often gathered through surveys, focus groups, or quite literally standing on the street corner asking people if they would buy your product or service! As an extension of your *Customer Profile* and the validation questions we looked at earlier, consider asking the following questions to drill down even deeper:

a. How much would you pay for this product/service?

b. Why would you buy this product/service?

c. Why wouldn't you buy this product/service?

d. From who, or where, do you currently buy similar products and services?

e. Is there anything you don't like about their products or services?

f. Where do you typically get information about products and services like these?

As a reminder, you can use a sales page online to test demand before creating your product or service – and this will help answer questions "a" and "b" above.

Once your primary and secondary research is concluded, write up an analysis in this section describing your findings and include all relevant conclusions drawn.

Competitor Analysis

Take the time to form a list of your primary competitors and research as much as you can about their companies. Factors to consider:

- **Product/service offerings**
- **Pricing**
- **Level of Customer Service**
- **Competitive Advantages – what makes them great?**
- **Competitive Disadvantages – what could they improve?**
- **Existing Market Share**
- **Customer Loyalty/Retention Rate**

You should then compile this information into a data table, like this:

	YOU	Competitor #1	Competitor #2
Products			
Price			
Customer Svc			
Comp Advantages			
Comp Disadvantages			
Market Share			
Customer Loyalty			

I recommend doing this in a spreadsheet for ease of comparison.

There are several places you can gather this information, and the two easiest places to do so are on **a competitor's website** and in **your competitor's sales department**!

Yes, that's right – you can simply call a competing company as though you're a potential customer and ask your questions down the line – *What are your product/service offerings? Pricing? Customer service?* And so on. This, by the way, is also a great way to research a company when pursuing it as a sales lead.

As you can imagine, someone on the inside sales team will be more than happy to fill you in on these details. For the sake of your karma, just don't waste *too* much of their time!

Now, in the event your line of business does not lend itself to such a scenario (for instance, if your primary competitors are sole proprietors working without a sales team), you may need to reach out to these individuals directly and ask for their honest advice.

What's worked for them and what hasn't? How did they come up with their current pricing? What changes have they made to their products or services and their marketing plan over time?

While it may seem awkward to ask a potential competitor for business advice, in the case of sole proprietors, most will be happy to share their experience with you.

Not to mention that having a discussion with someone who is already *doing* the work you're planning to do will give you a first-hand perspective of what your business will be like.

This provides you with a valuable opportunity to reaffirm your excitement for your idea, or reevaluate it if you hear something different from what you were expecting to hear. As an added bonus, partnership opportunities might even arise from such discussions, so stay positive during these interactions.

In Summary

It will take some time to answer the questions above and conduct all the research, but taking this seriously will give you the opportunity to identify potential threats to your business model, as well as unseen opportunities, before you hit the ground running.

7. Sales & Marketing Strategy

Your sales and marketing strategy is of vital importance, so you should plan to spend a significant amount of time on this part of your plan.

Everything else in your plan could look great, but if you don't have a viable means of connecting with customers, generating interest, and closing sales, you will fail to earn the revenue needed to keep the business afloat.

Having worked in sales for several years, I can tell you that there are a number of paths you can choose to take.

The trick is to identify the path that will be *most effective* for your business from both a results standpoint and an ROI (Return on Investment) standpoint.

Television commercials and freeway billboards may produce great results, but at what cost? Will you create enough revenue with those campaigns to justify the expense?

In order to learn as much as possible about sales, marketing, and ultimately gaining customer traction, I highly recommend reading a book called *Traction: How Any*

Startup Can Achieve Explosive Customer Growth by Gabriel Weinberg and Justin Mares.

In the book, they discuss nineteen different channels that can potentially be used – and which *should* be evaluated - for getting "traction" and ultimately closing sales with customers, regardless of the type of business you're in.

The nineteen channels include:

- SEO (Search Engine Optimization)
- SEM (Search Engine Marketing)
- Content Marketing
- Speaking Engagements
- PR (Public Relations)
- Unconventional PR
- Sales (Traditional Sales Methodologies)
- Business Development (Forming Partnerships)
- Engineering as Marketing
- Trade Shows
- Viral Marketing
- Email Marketing
- Social/Display Ads
- Offline Marketing
- Targeting Blogs
- Affiliate Programs
- Existing Platforms
- Offline Events
- Community Building

You should really get the book to dig into all the details, but the basic idea is, once you've settled on a business model, to evaluate all nineteen of these channels and choose a few at a time to "experiment" with to see how they pan out.

After some time, a winner can be chosen to focus on for a while and/or another group of potential traction channels can be tested in parallel.

Notably, Weinberg and Mares also point out that many times the most profitable channels are ones we do not initially consider viable.

For the purposes of your business plan, you may want to simply decide what you initially believe would be your top two or three channels and build your plan around those. If you ultimately elect to move forward with your plan, you can dig deeper into all of the many possibilities.

Since I have personal experience with sales, I'll break down the difference between Sales and Marketing (this is sometimes an area of confusion). These two words are very closely related, but the word *sales* is generally used to describe a more aggressive, outbound method of generating business, whereas *marketing* tends to focus on more passive, inbound methods of generating business.

Sales Funnel

- Lead Generation
- Lead Qualification
- Proposal/Quote
- Negotiation
- Close
- RM

Marketing Funnel

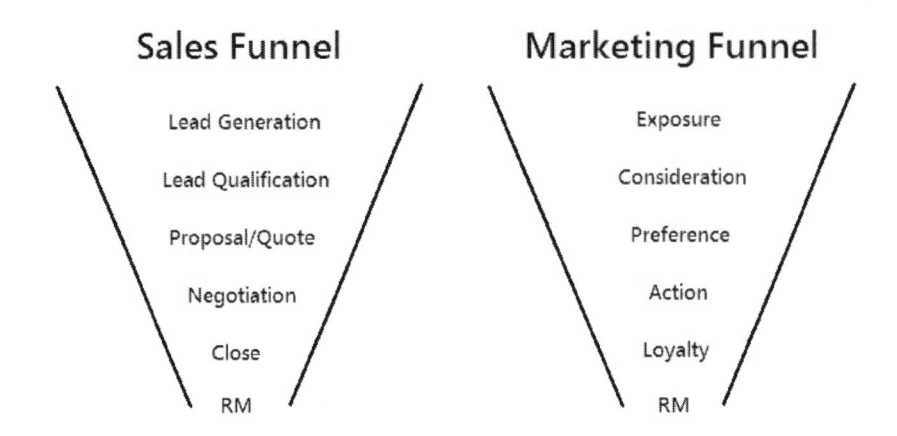

- Exposure
- Consideration
- Preference
- Action
- Loyalty
- RM

What is Sales?

Sales typically consists of *prospecting*, which includes making outbound cold calls, sending cold emails, or attending industry events (like trade shows) to form new relationships and generate *leads*.

The people who aren't even interested enough to talk to you should not be considered leads – and are unlikely to make it any farther down the sales funnel.

Those who express initial interest, or a willingness to learn more, are your actual leads. At this point, *qualification* involves asking your leads certain questions to determine if they are truly a good fit for your product or service.

Are they already getting a similar product from a competitor for a significantly lower rate? If so, this lead may not be qualified – and is unlikely to move farther down the funnel.

On the other hand, if you discover your lead is currently paying more for the competitor's product or that the competing product is inferior, you can likely consider the lead to be qualified.

Other questions to ask during qualification will be specific to your business, and should be aimed at determining whether or not the lead would benefit from your product or service.

For instance, if you are selling a software product that is primarily used by companies with at least 200-500 employees, you might ask your lead how many employees are currently working for the company.

Once you have determined that your lead is qualified, you can extend an offer in the form of a *proposal* or *price quote*.

Note that while price is important, it's never the only factor – many buyers would prefer to pay a little more for a superior product.

Whether your proposal comes in the form of an item sitting on the shelf (with a visible price tag) or in the form of a detailed PDF prospectus sent for your customer's review, your customer must have a chance to evaluate the price and features of your product or service before making a decision. It's important, therefore, to make sure you clarify these factors in enough depth for them.

Your customer may also want to *negotiate* the price or included features with you before moving forward.

Eventually, some percentage of the qualified leads to whom you send proposals will make a purchase – these are your *closed* deals.

These folks then move into the "RM" (relationship management/customer service) pool as *accounts* that you will hopefully retain for many years to come.

Please do keep in mind that at each stage of the funnel, you *will* lose people, and you need to manage your expectations properly to avoid getting bummed out about this.

At the very top of the funnel, there are people you talk to who just aren't interested at *all*, like we discussed. Then there are those who have some initial interest (or are too weak to tell you they aren't interested), but are not truly qualified – they don't have a current need or desire for your product or service. The ones who *do* have a need or desire for your product or service still need to evaluate their ability to make a purchase, and may decide the timing isn't right, that it's not in their budget, or that it's not a priority right now.

Therefore, you can count on losing plenty of people (or having them stall out) at each stage in the funnel, meaning you need to prospect for *lots and lots of people* at the top of the funnel to get just a few of them to the bottom.

Some people are more "cut out" for sales work than others, but it's a personal approach that continues to produce results for many successful companies and is certainly worth considering in your pursuit of traction.

What is Marketing?

Marketing is similar to sales, but unlike sales, it relies on a non-personal means of distributing your brand's message – think television ads, billboards, email marketing, email newsletters, bumper stickers, social media pages, magazine or newspaper ads, online marketing through Google AdWords or social channels, and more.

Marketing's passive nature can be a highly effective way of generating interest and ultimately moving people through your marketing funnel a little quicker. It can also be a way of generating leads for your sales team to close.

Instead of reaching out to people who might not be interested in your products and services, you will have people calling *in* to your business, asking for proposals or simply making purchases online if your marketing is effective.

Both businesspeople and customers like marketing because it's not as aggressive as sales, but keep in mind it comes at a high cost – running advertisements, building a website and email list, and paying for online services such as Google AdWords can add up fast.

By contrast, all a sales person needs to start building their pipeline is a list of potential leads, a telephone, and an email account – which is one reason I advocate this traction channel myself, even though it may not be right for everyone or effective for every business model.

At the end of the day, you'll need to evaluate what *you* believe is truly the most effective strategy for gaining customer traction at the outset (and throughout the growth) of your business.

Crafting Your Sales and Marketing Plan

Every business needs a strategy for gaining customer traction. Too many startups fail because they spend all their time, money, and resources in product development without ever determining how to bring their product to market and find paying customers.

Therefore, even if your business is largely focused on product development in the beginning, be sure to at least run some basic ads to gauge interest out in the marketplace.

Besides, your first customers, alpha/beta testers, and prospects (called "early adopters") will often tell you *exactly* what you need to know to develop a great product – and this is invaluable feedback during your early growth stages.

To determine the best places to run ads, think about your target market and where your potential customers are receiving their information about products and services like yours.

Is it mostly online? Through social media? Television? Friends and family (word of mouth)?

You need to figure this out to optimize the delivery of your advertisements to your target market – and if you don't figure this out in the beginning, you'll need to have a chunk of money set aside for experimentation and A/B testing in order to figure out what works when you launch your business.

Regardless of what direction you go with sales and marketing, you should estimate all costs associated with the strategies you plan to pursue and build them into your financial plan.

Here are a few examples of typical sales and marketing costs you can expect to encounter:

Common Marketing Costs

- Lead & Market Research
- Graphic Design
- A/B Experimentation
- Media Production
- Web Optimization & SEO
- Advertising
- Trade Show Exhibitor Fees

Common Sales Costs

- CRM Software (like Salesforce)
- Cell Phone and/or Company Car (for outside sales)

- Prospecting Lists
- Training (if you're hiring newbies)
- Trade Show Exhibitor Fees
- Fun Company Events, Bonuses, and Incentives (to keep salespeople motivated)

Keep in mind, too, that it takes time to build a customer pipeline regardless of what traction strategy you elect to pursue.

It is also likely that your first marketing campaigns will not be as effective as future campaigns. Strategies often require modification, tailoring, or abandonment in favor of other methods.

All this takes time, money, and patience – so remember to account for these factors up front. Give yourself the time to build, experiment, and grow. Budget some extra funds too, because you'll probably need them to experiment and ultimately determine the most profitable sales and marketing strategy.

To stay on track, it can help to organize your thoughts in a table for yourself, your business, and any investors or bankers looking at your business plan.

Sales & Marketing Data Table

	Cost/Month	Expected ROI	Time to Build
Niche Magazine Ad			
Online PPC Campaign			
Outbound Sales Calls			
Content Marketing			

Be sure to record your actual results over time so you can begin to measure what's working and what's not. This will give you the information you need to continually adapt, learn, and grow stronger with each passing day.

8. Operations & Logistics

This is where you must define how your business will operate on a daily basis. What are the moving pieces, and how do they fit together?

For instance, in the case of a t-shirt printing shop, you would need to discuss the location of your warehouse; list your potential suppliers of t-shirts, ink, and silkscreens; describe the turnaround time for supply orders and who will be responsible for coordinating them; discuss production methods, costs, and quality control; calculate daily output capacity; list any business licenses or permits required to operate; and more.

Every business model will have its own peculiarities, but generally speaking, this section should address the following topics in detail:

1. **Production/Operations**
    a. Raw Materials needed for production.
        i. List physical materials needed in the case of products.
        ii. List any certifications or licenses in the case of services.
    b. Suppliers – who will provide these things to the business?

c. Quality Control – what will be done to ensure output integrity?
   d. Production Methods – how will you create your deliverables?
   e. Inventory Management (if applicable).

2. **Staff/HR**
   a. Job Descriptions.
   b. Hiring Strategy.
   c. Compensation.
   d. Organizational Structure – who does what, how will employees work together, who will have authority over whom?
   e. Company Procedures.
   f. Schedules.

3. **Legal/Administrative**
   a. Licenses and Permits – at the local, county, state, federal, and trade organization level.
   b. Conformity to Government Regulations.
   c. Insurance.
   d. Workplace Laws, such as OSHA.
   e. Intellectual Property – copyrights, patents, or trademarks.
   f. Legal Advice – who will you contact or retain?

4. **Financial**
    a. Accounting Methods.
    b. Reporting Requirements.
    c. Taxes – Payment of Franchise Tax, Sales & Use Tax, and any other specialty or excise taxes.
    d. Creation of Company Financial Accounts – also list anyone authorized to make transactions on behalf of the business.
    e. Company Credit Policies – Will you extend credit terms to customers or require prepayment? What policies will be in place to govern this?
    f. Management of Accounts Receivable and Accounts Payable.
    g. Accountant/CPA – who will you retain for financial advice?

If you're a one-man or –woman show, you might be thinking that all this looks to be a little irrelevant for you.

The hard truth of the matter is that all these areas still apply to a sole proprietor and must be given the proper consideration when starting a legitimate business.

In the case of a blog or website, for example, the content you are producing is your "production," and your "raw materials" might include the research you do for your posts. Your "suppliers" would be your domain host, content management service (like WordPress), and email-marketing partners (like AWeber, Constant Contact, or Zoho).

Your "staff" will be *you*, and you sure better come up with a schedule for generating content. On the legal side, you'll need to ensure you avoid issues by not posting copyrighted images, and on the financial side, you'll need to discuss how you'll keep track of earnings and pay your taxes.

Now let me tell you a story, to give you some extra motivation to spend the proper time crafting your operational plan regardless of how big or small your business may be.

When I started my first business, giving guitar lessons in college, I took the time to report my income (mostly cash) on my tax return. A full three years after my last year of reporting, I received a letter from San Diego county indicating that I'd failed to obtain a permit required to conduct business and owed hundreds of dollars in fines and penalties, *and* was possibly guilty of a misdemeanor!

Fortunately, I turned on the paralegal part of my brain, started doing some research, and was able to identify an exemption that I qualified for under the law. After I wrote a letter to the county, requesting this exemption and explaining my basis for qualification, they dropped the matter altogether. Had I not qualified for the exemption, though, it could have been a real pain in the neck to sort out.

Most new entrepreneurs learn things like this the hard way. No one tells us we need a certain permit or license (or we never take the time to do our due diligence to find out, as I am suggesting you do), and it eventually catches up to us as a big surprise.

It's best to minimize surprises by doing your homework up front.

Therefore, **be *proactive* and research these things ahead of time**. Hire an attorney or accountant to provide professional advice if needed. I've learned to do this when confronting areas of uncertainty, and it's given me great peace of mind.

9. Management Structure

Let's keep this one simple, because it is. Make a list of the following persons, as applicable:

- Owners
- Board of Directors
- C-Level Executives (CEO, CFO, COO)
- Managers
- Supervisors

You may also wish to list any outside, independent contractors involved with key aspects of your business such as:

- Attorneys
- Accountants
- Investor Advisors
- Business Consultants
- Financial Advisors

Last but not least, if your business will have several employees, provide an organizational chart like the one below. At a minimum, specify who will have authority over whom.

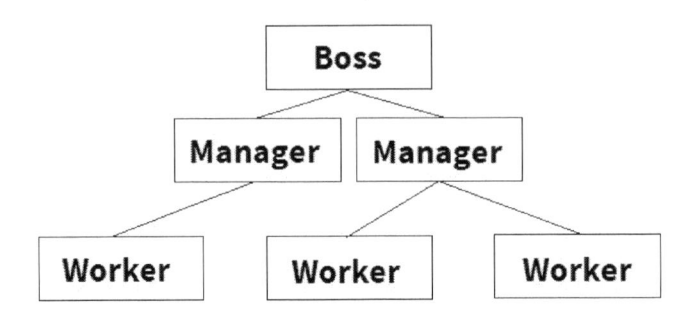

24-Hour Business Plan Template – Management Structure

```
                    ┌─────────┐
                    │  Boss   │
                    └─────────┘
                   ╱           ╲
          ┌───────────┐   ┌───────────┐
          │  Manager  │   │  Manager  │
          └───────────┘   └───────────┘
             ╱          ╱        ╲
    ┌──────────┐  ┌──────────┐  ┌──────────┐
    │  Worker  │  │  Worker  │  │  Worker  │
    └──────────┘  └──────────┘  └──────────┘
```

10. Business Capitalization

This is where you list your *startup costs* and describe how those costs will be covered in the beginning. Money might come from investors, a bank loan, or straight out of your pocket.

Common startup costs include:

- **Business Registration & Licensing**
- **Professional Legal & Financial Advice and Assistance**
- **Communications & Network Expenses** (Internet, Phones…)
- **Web Hosting, Design, and Development**
- **PP&E – Property, Plant, and Equipment**
- **Utilities, Trash, and Water**
- **Initial Inventory**
- **Insurance & Bonding**
- **Logo Design & Marketing Materials**
- **Starting Payroll**
- **Miscellaneous Expenses**

Be sure to conduct thorough research into *all* of your costs and then build in some padding for good measure (it's best to do this as a separate line item, although if you want, you can pad each individual expense listed). It's very common to underestimate startup costs, and you'll want this padding to ensure your business can still reach its goals if things wind up costing a little more than planned.

11. Financial Plan

Here we will review two aspects of your financial plan: the *business* financial plan and your *personal* financial plan. We'll keep this simple, but be sure you spend adequate time thinking through realistic profit-and-loss projections when conducting this exercise for your business.

Business Financial Plan

This plan should include:

1. **Financial Snapshot upon Launch**
   This is your Day One opening balance sheet. It should list the amount of cash in the bank, what's already been spent on equipment or supplies, any assets or inventory of the business, and all existing liabilities (such as bank loans).

2. **One-Year Profit Projection**
   This is how you project your business will be doing after one year. It should list the same metrics as in the financial snapshot above, but also provide an explanation of how the business will get there. What things need to happen to reach this point and how will you ensure that these things happen? What sales volume must the business achieve, what costs will the business incur, and under what assumptions

are you working to derive your estimates? Are those assumptions safe and conservative or risky and aggressive?

3. **Five-Year Profit Projection**
   This is the same as the one-year projection, but carried out further into the future.

4. **Estimated Cash Flow**
   This is where you get to stack up all your monthly expenses – payroll, rent, related bills, supply costs, and so on – and compare them with your expected monthly revenues (the money your business earns from selling its products and services).

   Your monthly break-even point will be easy to calculate once you have an accurate estimate of all your monthly expenses, including payroll and your own pay.

   Since cash flow is the life-blood of your business, you should also show how long your initial operating capital will last in the event you operate at a loss for a period of time.

   For example, if your business starts with **$25,000** in the bank and your expected monthly cash flow is ($3,000) for the first three months, ($1,500) for the next six months, and ($500) for the next three months, this initial operating capital will be reduced by $19,500 in the first year, leaving you with just $5,500. At that point, hopefully it is your projection that monthly cash flow will at least break even, if not turn positive, since there will be very little capital left to keep the business afloat if it continues to operate at a loss.

Remember, when the money in the bank runs out and the business can no longer pay its bills, the game is over. So it's best to be conservative here (underestimate profitability, if anything) to minimize the chance of running into a cash flow bind once the business is already up and running.

Personal Financial Plan

Your personal financial plan details how you will cover your expenses during the startup period of your business.

In the event you are borrowing money from investors or a bank, you will need to list your current personal assets and liabilities along with your net worth. It may be necessary to provide copies of tax returns from the past few years as well.

If you are a sole proprietor going into business for yourself, I would recommend going through the following exercise as well:

24-Hour Business Plan Template – Financial Plan

1. Identify the startup capital required to launch your business.
2. Examine your cash-flow projections to determine how many months or years it will take to become profitable.
3. Add in a buffer and nail down a final number, showing how much money you will need in the bank to make this happen.
4. Now compare this amount of money to what you currently have in the bank. Do you already have what you need, or do you need more money?
5. If you need more money, how much and how will you get it?
    - Evaluate these five options for raising the required capital:

        - **Raise it yourself** – Calculate how many months you will need to continue working at your current job to come up with this amount. Is this length of time acceptable? If so, great! To accelerate the process, identify ways you can cut back on your existing expenses and stick to your plan.

        - **Find a business partner** – If you're willing to split the profit on your business, finding a business partner who is willing to contribute to the capitalization of the business is a great way to accelerate things.

- **Ask the bank**! – Getting a bank loan can be a great option when you need a considerable sum of money that would otherwise take you too long to drum up elsewhere. However, be cautious since you will likely need to sign a personal guarantee allowing the bank to pursue you for your own personal assets in the event your business does not succeed. This is true even if you form an LLC or corporation. You better feel confident in your business plan if you go this route!

- **Find an investor** – Whether it's an angel investor willing to throw several hundred thousand dollars at your wild idea or a more conservative investor who believes in your ability to succeed, this can be a great option since everybody wins when your business succeeds. And if the business does not succeed, you will not have a bank after you for your personal assets – the investor generally accepts the loss.

- **Ask a friend or family member** – If the amount required is small and it will save you many months or years of waiting, asking a friend or family member to lend you a few thousand dollars (or more) might be the answer. Only you can know if this is possible or appropriate, however.

V. Conclusion

There you have it – you're done with your business plan!

As I mentioned at the start of this book, I used the format, layout, and process in this book to plan and launch my own full-time business in a matter of months.

I know you can do the same if you get focused and make this happen, and I'd love nothing more than to hear about your progress along the way.

Please also consider leaving an honest review of this book online. Whether you loved it or not, it would be great to hear your sincere feedback!

As a reminder, there are some templates and accompanying resources available at no cost on my website that will accelerate the process for you:

http://www.stevenfies.com/24-hour-business-plan-template

If you have any questions about this book or the concepts within it, please feel free to reach out to me via my website. It would be a pleasure for me to help you in your quest to launch your business and become an entrepreneur.

For now, cheers!

Made in the USA
San Bernardino, CA
27 June 2016